THE WHITE WOLF DADDY (BLOOD BATH)

By:Anthony Hawkins

ISBN:978-1-312-88987-3

Dedicated to the gay and lesbian community.

Warning:This book contains graphic explicit and mature content.

Prologue

It was a dark night on a snowy day in the countrysides,and i was on the hunt,i had tracked this coven of vampires who had kidnapped a young 8 year old african american boy,in order to drain him of his blood,his pure young blood.

Many vampires enjoyed the taste of a childs blood due to it being fresh and not yet too tainted by smoking or drugs,the blood of druggies was unappetizing to them.

As im walking the snowy sidewalk with my long trench coat waving in the cold breeze i catch the scent of fresh blood,then look down to see crimson red blood trailing into the woods,some of it belonging to a young caucasian woman,and some of it belonging to a young boy around the age of 4,they were both dead,their clothes covered in their own blood.

The wolf in me wanted to get a taste of their blood,but i fought it off,me being a werewolf gave me cravings i would never crave as an average man,but that was not the case.

The world as we know it has many worlds beyond that,the world of the supernatural,werewolfs,vampires,wit ches,and much much more,most unseen by human eyes,most being myth and legend to them.

But to me the supernatural was all too familiar,and well known,i myself was a part of the supernatural world,me being a werewolf,having all the powers a werewolf in legend or myth would possess,but none of the weaknesses.

The cries of a young boy caught my ears as i moved in closer deep into the woods,the cries belonged to the young african american boy.

Three men surrounded the young black boy as they held him in their grips,the men being vampires.

The men gave me glares of caution,warning me to stay back from them,but i just politely told them to give me the boy.

Please my good men,just give me the boy,and i'll go away,this one has caught my interest for some reason,i spoke calmly to the three men,the vampire men then chuckling in response.

You just want to feed on him yourself werewolf,we could catch your scent a mile away,now leave us before we make you our next meal punk,one of the three men spoke rudely to me,then showing his fangs as they extended from his gums.

The young boy gave me an innocent look as if he didn't know why these men were doing this to him,he didn't know why these men wanted his blood,but then as me and the boy stared eye to eye silently,one of the vampires leaned down in to bite him,but before his teeth could pierce into the boys flesh i had lunged over to him,and ripped off his head with my own fangs as blood now covered them,vampire blood.

The vampires headless body then fell to the snow limp as i tossed his detached blood dripping head into the bushes,the other vampires then quickly fleeing the young boy as they thought they too would soon be headless like their comrade laying next to me.

I gently took the boy into my grip,and then headed home,my home,and soon to be his home as well,if he wanted to stay.

Later on that week i found out why i was so drawn to the young black boy,his great great grandmother was my lover once,a beautiful human african american woman named Jeniece,his scent was similiar to hers,him being one of her descendants,Jeniece had died of old age,and refused to let me turn her,werewolves didn't age,just the same as vampires,i've lived for a very long time,way past two centuries.

The boys name was Jomonte,he told me once he began to warm up to me,the young black boy i tracked now had a name to go with his face.I kept Jomonte hidden from the supernatural world,not wanting him to get involved in it,and it's dangers,but he was growing fast,and soon he would want to see the world,the entire world,including the supernatural.

I was a tall six foot two handsome caucasian man with german roots,had dark wavy hair,and a set of caramel brown colored eyes,i had a strong lean and very toned and sculpted physique,my face square shaped,and my jaws strong and high,my skin peachy colored with a radiant bronze glow to it,my name is Tobias.

Jomonte knew we were different in many ways,but he still accepted me as his comrade,and i raised him as a father would a son,tho i was more of a mentor to him,a very good friend.

Chapter 1

11 years passed,and Jomonte had grown into a handsome young 20 year old man,still living with me

faithfully in my huge house that could fit an army or small village.

It was a friday night,and i could hear Jomonte in the other room going through the change,the change of becoming a werewolf,i myself had turned Jomonte after he had been attacked by a thirsty vampire on a late night as he was coming home from the local movie theater in town,the werewolf change healed his wounds he had previously received from the vampire,and he was soon just like me,a werewolf,a part of the supernatural.

Jomonte enjoyed being a werewolf,except for the cravings of fresh blood,but all in all he enjoyed it,the heightened speed,strength,agility,and the accelerated healing,but he didn't make a full werewolf shift just yet,he was still quite new to his new powers and abilities,but i was going to teach him,as i always did,and was proud of doing.

Come with me Jomonte,let's go outside for a stroll in the forest,i have much to show you,much,i spoke warmly to Jomonte as i fetched a coat from the coatrack,and placed it around my fully clothed body,Jomonte then placing on his coat as well,and then both of us leaving our home together,the cool breeze hitting us as we exited,tho we did not get cold,our body temperatures being much higher than the average humans,but we still kept appearances,in able to blend in with the rest of the human world,tho we were from both human and supernatural worlds.

Me and Jomonte headed through the woods side by side,but then stopped near an open field.

Now,i want you to try and change right here,make a full wolf shift,you can do it,if i can,you can,i spoke to Jomonte in confidence he could indeed do it.

I dont think i can do it Tobias,i swear i cant,Jomonte spoke to me in self doubt,but i refused to believe he couldn't make the full change,because i knew he could,with the right push.

Let your anger and emotion and need to be something else take over you for just a split second,and then you'll feel yourself making the change,you'll feel yourself becoming wolf and man,a full werewolf,i explained to Jomonte carefully as he listened.

I then began to partially change myself,showing Jomonte how to control his werewolf transformation,as i turned my eyes a shimmering neon gold,and then my claws extending from my fingernails as my canine teeth slightly extended from my gums in a half werewolf transformation,Jomonte watching me the entire time,taking mental notes.

Suddenly as i reverted back into my human form i caught the sound of footsteps approaching me and Jomonte,then as i turned toward the sound i saw a pair of bright crimson red eyes staring at me and Jomonte through the trees,pure hatred and anger in them,hunger as well.

The red eyes belonged to a pale skin man dressed in a suit and long trench coat,a man who was indeed a vampire,and then suddenly another pair of crimson red eyes came through the trees,these eyes belonging to a female vampire fully clothed in a trench coat as well,a female who was probably the other vampires mate.

Both the male and female vampires watched me and Jomonte as we stared back at them with caution.

Jomonte i think it's time for us to go,let's head home now,i spoke to Jomonte,wanting to get far away from the vampires as soon as possible,without making it too obvious.

Just as me and Jomonte turned to leave,i felt a hand touch my shoulder in a flash,the hand was cold as ice,the hand of the undead,the hand of the vampire man.

Chapter 2

What's the rush? Me and my beautiful girlfriend were just searching for a nice spot to dine,and i think we've found it,the vampire man spoke to me smugly as his fangs extended from his gums and headed for my neck,but in a quick flash i tossed the vampire from me in one quick sweeping movement of my arm,the vampire flinging into the air but then catching his balance as he landed on his feet.

I like when my food is spicy and lively,makes it much tastier to eat,the vampire man spoke to me and Jomonte with a smirk as he showed his fangs to us,the female vampire then showing hers as well as both her and the man began to approach me and Jomonte.

Leave us,me and my comrade will go in peace,i spoke to the vampires,but they still approached,the male after me,but the female soon turning her sight to Jomonte,her red eyes gleaming with thirst.So in a quick bound i shoved the female vampire away from Jomonte,standing over her as my own fangs escaped my gums in anger.

The male vampire then leaped on top of me,knocking me over onto the grass of the woods,as he tried to pierce me with his fangs in thirst,he had the advantage at first,until i could feel the heat and rage and adrenaline flowing throughout my body changing me from man to beast,and then soon my fingernails extended into claws that began to pierce into the flesh of the vampire mans arm,and then soon i could feel my body becoming more exposed to the open air,as my clothes began to peel from the new size and strength of my growing and morphing body,the vampire now having fear in his eyes,the vampire now knowing i wasn't quite fully human myself,i was a part of the supernatural,a werewolf,and they hadn't caught my scent until now.

The vampire man tried to pin me down further,but he was no match for my growing strength,as i shoved him from me and then leaped on top of him still peeling out of my clothes as i changed into a full huge seven foot tall wolf,my canines showing sharply.

Just as my full wolf shift was coming to completion the female vampire began to charge toward me with the intent to kill me,but in a lighting fast bound i saw Jomonte rip from out of his clothes from his new size in a full wolf transformation landing violently on top of the female vampire to protect me from her attack,his body naked as trails of brown fur that was just as brown as his radiant skin trailed down his abdomen and then down to his sex organs,encasing them in a patch of fur,his claws sharp and long,his canines sharp and deadly,a deep growl releasing from his snout in anger at the vampire laying under him in his strong grip.

The vampire man desperately tried to escape my grasp as he saw his female mate in danger,my body continuing the full wolf shift as my clothes fell from my naked body,vanilla white fur trailing down my underbelly and my face,my canines showing,and my claws pressing deeply into the mans flesh through his clothes as i snarled at him angrily in a deep beastly growl,blood then soaking them as it leaked from the wounds my claws caused the man.

The vampire man then shrieked out in pain as my claws grew deeper into his flesh,then my canines going for his neck as i sunk them deeply into it,then jerking my head to the left as i ripped the vampire mans head off,crimson red blood spewing from the stump of his detached head,his body still laying under me as it was headless.

And then i turned to Jomonte to check in on him,seeing him swiftly rip the vampire womans head off her body,her head then rolling to the side as i caught it in my sharp canines,slinging it next to her dead mates,both their bodies headless and lifeless,tho they weren't completely dead,vampires could heal just as fast as us werewolves could,and took quite the effort to kill.

I helped Jomonte tear the vampire woman apart with our canines and claws,i first tore off one of her arms,as Jomonte tore off the other one,then we both tore off her legs,leaving only a bloody torso,then after we fully dismembered the female,we moved onto the male,doing the same to him as well,then afterwards we flung the vampires remains into a nearby lake,disposing of them,the lake water turning red with vampires blood for awhile in a small section,but then washing down the stream.

Me and Jomonte ran through the woods in our wolf forms side by side as we headed home from the blood bath as the trees passed us by quickly in our immense super human speed,we got thrills from it,the speed was like our own drug,and we enjoyed it together,as our own wolf pack of two.

Chapter 3

Me and Jomonte reverted back into our human forms once we reached home,our bodies naked and covered in the vampires blood,our clothes left behind in the woods torn into shreds from our previous change,serving no more use to us.

I guess a higher emotional push was all you needed to make the full werewolf change my boy,you did it,i told you you could,and i thank you for your bold choice in trying to protect me back there,theres honor in that,come,let's wash up now,i spoke to Jomonte proudly as we both headed inside together,Jomonte giving me a warm smile in return,as i returned the favor.

Me and Jomonte twisted on the showerheads in two seperate shower stalls of the huge master bath inside,and then began to clean ourselves of all the vampire blood as we soaped up under the hot raining showerheads,the water beating against our naked bodies,steam filling the room.

Both me and Jomonte placed clean short white above knee length towels around the waists of our naked bodies once we were through with our hot showers,then sliding our feet into shower shoes as we exited the steam filled master bath,our toned bodies walking side by side in nothing but the short towels around our waists as we headed down the hall together like a wolf and it's pup.

Both me and Jomonte stopped as we got near the huge window that was lit with moonlight shining through in the open living area,our toned bodies still standing side by side,the short towels around our naked waists grazing as we stared at the moon outside the huge window together in an intimate moment.

Tho some would see me as a father figure or guardian to Jomonte,i saw him for the first time in a new light,an intimate and romantic way to be precise,the way his gorgeous smooth brown skin and pecks and smooth abs and his toned legs that protruded from the above knee length towel around the waist of his naked body looked very seductive and enticing and new to me,i desired him,i was like a male dog in heat,and it scared me somewhat at first,Jomonte reminded me so much of Jeniece.

Romance had no color or gender,and i was learning that all so well,as i stared over at Jomonte with hot arousal coursing through my body,my loins stiffening in secret as we stood side by side,the short towels around our naked waists still grazing a bit,the setting was romantic and in some ways seductive.

Jomonte caught me staring at him,and then gave me a warm stare back,a silent and smooth intimate stare,as if he was feeling the same way i was,but should i make the first move on him was the question i asked myself? Did Jomonte actually see me the way i saw him at that moment,or would my romantic gestures push him away,did he only see me as his guardian or father,his white wolf daddy?

Two wolf men staring at the moon,the night is beautiful,my young pup has grown,i gently placed my arm around Jomonte warmly.Yeah,i guess i have man,Jomonte spoke back to me warmly,and then placing his arm around me as well,the above knee towels around our naked waists touching as our bare sides touched also,our warm flesh meeting each other in an intimate and touching moment between men.

You know,when wolves find their mates they know it,they get this feeling,an intense feeling,many call it the mating call,or imprinting,but imprinting can mean many things,i turned to Jomonte intimately,as we stared eye to eye,not breaking contact.

Soon i then eased my lips to Jomonte's,kissing him softly,and then swinging my arms around him gently,as we both embraced intimately and romantically,our lips touching,our exposed chests meeting,the short white towels around the waists of our sculpted and toned naked bodies grazing,and our thighs and knees and legs mingling,and the shower shoes on our feet clashing.

Jomonte kissed me back with just as much passion as i did him,and we both reveled in it,the soft sound of the flesh of our lips meeting continuously without pause in deep lust and passion.

I slid my tongue into Jomonte's mouth inbetween his smooth full lips as we continued to kiss in deep passion and thrill,Jomonte then doing

the same,our kiss insane with lust
and need.

My strong hands began to trace up
and down Jomonte's smooth back,as
we still embraced lip to lip,Jomonte's
fingers then caressing my neck and
the back of my head.

Me and Jomonte then eased
ourselves to the area rug below us as
we still continued to kiss
passionately,our kiss giving noise
throughout the silent house,our
hands groping each other smoothly.

I positioned myself on top of Jomonte
as we continued to kiss hot lips to hot

lips,chest to chest,short towel to short towel,thigh to thigh,knee to knee,naked exposed flesh to naked exposed flesh,my peachy bronze flesh to his chocolate brown flesh hotly and intimately.

I soon took the short white towel off the waist of my strong naked body,as i then unwrapped the short white towel from around the waist of Jomonte's naked body as well,both me and Jomonte's fully naked radiant smooth bodies now in the open,the open air beating against our exposed naked flesh lightly as we began to kiss again harshly in deep lust,our eyes enjoying the raw nakedness of each others bodies.

Me and Jomonte then smoothly joined our flesh together in a gasp of pleasure as we felt our naked flesh and sexual organs intertwine down below in pleasure,our loins squeezing and plunging inbetween and back and forth together intertwined in intense sexual pleasure,as we both rocked up and down together on the area rug in our hot nakedness,our faces giving away the excitement and gratification we felt.

Me and Jomonte then soon jerked our naked bodies up and down and back and forth with more passion and rhythm as we felt our loins dig deeper into lustful pleasure,our flesh locking tightly together as we felt ourselves pulsing and quivering down below from the inside,my flesh touching Jomonte in the right pleasure spots,as his touched mine.

In the middle of me and Jomonte's love making we began to kiss again,our lips meeting hotly as our naked flesh did,our bodies thrusting in pleasure as Jomonte caressed and groped my smooth round exposed buttocks and back as we became lost in our hot lust and sexual pleasure in a hot pit of our naked smooth flesh.

Me and Jomonte made love for hours,until we both began to feel our loins heat up in deep pleasure of our intense love making.

Me and Jomonte rocked our smooth hot naked bodies together one last time as we felt our connected loins down below heat up and fill with the ultimate climax of our sexual satisfaction,and then soon we both erupted in an intense heated orgasm and ejaculation of passion and deep pleasure as it passed throughout our loins hotly,and strongly,deep moans of sexual completion and gratification escaping both me and Jomonte's lips as they met with strong impact once again after our orgasmic hot and wet explosion of pleasure,our bodies filled and soaked with our orgasm.

Me and Jomonte panted back and forth in sexual relief and release and pleasure,and then soon our eyes closing to sleep,as we slept together in our nakedness holding each other tightly throughout the rest of the night,as new mates.

I loved Jeniece dearly,and never thought i would find another,but Jomonte was just like a male version

of Jeniece,and i loved him,but unlike
Jeniece,he would be with me
forever,and ever,throughout eternity.

The end

www.ingramcontent.com/pod-product-compliance
Lightning Source LLC
Chambersburg PA
CBHW050351290526
45785CB00006B/2726